Toolkit For Success

7 Tools to Manifest the Life of Your Dreams

by Veronica Hurst

Table of Contents:

Chapter 1: page 4
You Only Have One

Chapter 2: page 15
Simplify Your Life

Chapter 3: page 25
Prioritize Your Life

Chapter 4: page 30
Live Outside Your Comfort Zone

Chapter 5: page 43
The Golden Rule

Chapter 6: page 48
Always Keep Learning

Chapter 7: page 51
Living With Gratitude

All contents copyrighted and protected by law. No reproduction or use of content without permission from the author.

Chapter 1: You Only Have One

You only have one life.

Life is beautiful and many people's wish in life tend to be that they could relax more, cherish life and ultimately have even just a little more time.

When we move through life, we focus a lot on our goals and how our life is developing. We want to make sure that we accomplish all of that we set out to do and we want to become successful and financially stable.

We want a good life. We want to be treated with respect and praised for our self expression and who we are as a person.

But the truth is, we tend to get locked into our survival modes and life passes us by in a blink of an eye. So what do we do in order to cherish our life?

In order to really create a life that you truly live to the fullest, you need to address the major laws that govern your emotions. The perfect model to address this is through Maslow's Hierarchy of Needs.

Maslow's Hierarchy of Needs.

Whether you like it or not, Maslow's Hierarchy of Needs heavily impacts you and your life. By making sure you master these important necessities inside of life you'll be able to move on to a more inspirational life.

Odds are that if you're stressed, it's due to your lack of one of these stages. It's important to fill these needs so you can move on to what truly matters. Making your life incredible.

So what are the Hierarchy of Needs?

The hierarchy is like a giant and powerful pyramid of human instincts and it works like this!

5. The bottom of the pyramid is the foundation of your life and your most basic human emotions. It is the drive for what your body needs to keep you alive. From food, water and sleep all the way to movements and activities.

-Sometimes money plays a role when it comes to the bottom of the pyramid because it directly messes with one of the most fundamental principles inside of your body, your homeostasis. If you're financially stressed, you might focus on loosing your house, and your lack of shelter which could ultimately lead to lack of food, sleep and safe water.

-Also, a terrible diet filled with sugar and empty

carbs as well as well as insomnia, lack of learning or exercise directly effect your basic foundations inside of your life and throw you out of whack.

4. Next up on the pyramid is security. This area includes shelter from the dangerous wild. This can include dangerous and unstable living conditions that can send your life into turbulence.

-When you have internal conflicts, the feelings of security will be trying to overpower your efforts towards action. A simple way to move through this is by ensuring your emotion that what you're doing is secure. Really dive in and explain exactly how you're keeping your life and your body secure while you're going for a more successful life.

3. The middle of the pyramid is not surprisingly social. The needs include a sense of belonging and love. Over the course of our evolution, people found out that it was important to stick together. When people ventured off by themselves throughout the course of time, they tended to die. This left our ancestors with the innate sense of needing to live in groups. Everyone who ventured off alone died out and everyone who stuck together evolved leaving us with the powerful need to be a part of our community.

It's OK to cruise through this stage on your way to success. A perfect way to have a sense of love and belonging is to stay in touch with your friends and family every once in a while and by really connecting with people that have the same dreams and passions as you. This will give you a perfect sense of belonging and will allow you to focus on your goals in life. If you don't feel like you belong in your current set of relationships, surround yourself with people who share the same sense of aspiration. If you can't find anyone in your direct city or friend group, then cruise online. There are plenty of people who are passionate about the same things as you are. Give it time and you'll eventually surround yourself with the right people! Just make sure that if you don't have it now, join a few forums and social groups online. That'll get you started and keep you happy during your journey to success.

4. Once we find a nice groove of security in our environment, the top of the pyramid starts to focus on personal needs. The 4th Hierarchy of Need is all about the ego. People have a need to be accepted by the group that they are in because to our ancestors, getting booted out of the group traditionally meant that you would die. People heavily value the opinions of others and if you believe that you're causing turmoil inside of your environment's life, you'll begin to have an extreme dose of internal conflict.

A perfect way to solve this ego problem is to casually drop things to your family and loved ones. Don't make your goals and passions a big deal unless the support you and dive in. This will let others support you while giving you the freedom to pursue your dreams of becoming successful!

5. **The last stage of the pyramid is success**.

Yup! Until you conquer the first 4 stages, you'll consistently encounter self sabotaging, self doubt and inner conflict. But after you get a grasp on your other 4 stages of life, you'll be able to naturally focus on success and expand into your full potential.

Once you understand the 4 basic needs of you life, you become naturally in tune to becoming successful and it becomes an incredible part of your life. If you eat right, sleep well and put yourself in the correct environment with people that support your passions, you'll naturally be able to focus on your goals and dreams.

The truth is that even though everybody knows this, life is short.

It's important to master you basic needs for the emotions that drive you so you can spend your life doing something incredible and by doing something you love.

Life is short isn't actually a figure of speech. We have a limited time spent on this Earth and a lot of people tend to spend it worrying about keeping other people happy and keeping their life in order instead of going for it.

People's number one regret in life is wishing they would have done more in the life that they were given. But when we imagine a goal and a dream, we tend to cause friction in our environment and our Ego based hierarchy sabotages our moves for success. And instead of fighting other people for our rights to success, we should try to find a balance.

Never fight against the Hierarchy because they contain our most powerful emotions and fuel our survival. Always build on your Hierarchy instead of ripping it apart.

We only have one life and it's important to use it by focusing on what truly matters in life. Living a life you truly love. Without doing this, you'll be left with very little when the time comes.

Stand up for your right to pursue your dreams but do it for yourself. Do it internally. Keep your dreams quiet and let your Hierarchy work for you instead of against you.

When you do this, your life comes more naturally and success and transformation inside of your life is practically inevitable rather than practically impossible.

Life is Short

Life is short. Ask yourself what you really want to spend your time on this Earth.

How do you truly want to live your life and how do you want to be remembered?

An average life holds an average of 22,075,000 seconds. This might seem like a lot and that leaves us over 25,000 days throughout our life. If that seems like a lot, think about it this way. Yeah that's all good and stuff; but the truth is, if you're anywhere close to 30, you've already lived close to 10,000 days and if you're about 20 you've lived about 7,500 days out.

So, the clock is actually ticking a little more quickly than what you realized.

Humans have very few moments in life where they have that an epiphany.

These epiphanies are rare but they allow us to look at our lives and change it to send our lives in a direction we want. Then we get back to work with our daily lives and life cruises on by naturally until we have another epiphany.

These chances are incredibly rare inside of our moments in life but the power of a simple epiphany can transform your life forever.

Every day you spend is another one gone and before you know it, your week is gone and time comes around to pay for your home and your bills.

So where do you see yourself heading if your current track continues?

You only do live once so how'd you truly like to spend it, where would you like to go and what would you like to do with your life?

You live in a cycle of habits and life is no doubt wonderful. But be careful not to let it pass you by.

Live Passionately

Sadly, it's known that most employees dread going to work throughout their life.
There is a fine line between work and play and when the weekend is up, they go back to their office desk and hit the computer for 8 hours of busy work.
But the truth is, successful people tend to not know the difference between work and play. They love waking up and getting to work and it's not because they are super nerds or that they working away their life.
It's because they live with their life with passion and they spend their lives doing what they love.
If you're looking to become successful and you're not exactly sure why you can't get a handle on working hard, maybe you should approach work from a different way or maybe with time, you should find a different job or start a business on what you love.
The truth is, the super successful have quite a few fancy hacks, but passion is one of the most incredible. It automatically leads to higher quality work, better productive and creates undivided attention.
Sometimes, when you follow your passions, you end up getting a little bit of backlash from people who don't understand exactly what's happening. But not everyone is passionate about the same exact thing so it's ok to believe in yourself and follow your passion when you begin your journey towards becoming successful. Not everybody will see eye to eye with you about every subject in life but it's a well known gem among the successful.
There are millions of ways to make money in this world and to create an income so what's the point of generating an income in a way that you don't like?

Money and passion don't always go hand in hand but the successful in any industry love what the do 9 times out of 10.
So what's your passion in life and how can you use that to build an income?
If you're still a bit skeptical of the power of passion, here's a few ways a little bit of it will transform your life.

1. Passion give you motivation during the most troubling times.

Sometimes, your goals and dreams get ridiculously tough and can even seem impossible. But having a passion for what you're doing will give you the drive to keep going and to spend time on finding solutions instead of giving up. When you're passionate about a subject and something isn't working you have the natural ability to drive innovation and to create new ideas for your goals and business. Without passion, when you hit major obstacles on your journey to success; you'll feel like it's better just to hang up the towel and come back to it later on.

2. Passion creates curiosity and curiosity sparks learning.

When you spark curiosity, you tend to learn a lot of new things and you retain what you learn a lot better. As you dive into your passions, you immerse yourself inside of systems and strategies and your mind begins to engage with what you're learning. Once your mind engages and interacts with what you're working on, your ideas become fun and produce creative ideas that will give you an advantage as your goals develop over time.
Never loos your senses of wonder and curiosity. When you grow up and learn that you have

responsibilities, grown ups tend to loose that sense of marvel and that's natural. However, that keen sense of curiosity and passion is what fuels the world's greatest minds.

3. Passion is contagious.

Your passion is contagious when you bring it to the table. While not everyone will respond, people love to engage and be entertained. It's within our nature and even accountants and lawyers love the ability to make work more fun.

People are naturally drawn to charisma and passion because it's attractive in an otherwise boring life. When you really dive in and get excited throughout your work, other people will take notice.
When you become passionate, you also tend to draw out other passions inside of people and attract the types of people you need inside of your life to succeed.
Passion connects with passion and there's a lot of benefits to networking with incredibly passionate people. You'll be amazed at what you learn through curiosity and enjoyment on your journey to success.

4. Passion leads to enjoyment.

If you truly love what you're doing, you'll enjoy work day in and out. Instead of going to work begrudgingly, you'll begin to naturally dive in after you got some rest and you'll love every minute of it. Remember the fact that life is finite and time is scarce so why not spend it enjoying yourself?
Not every part about every job is entertaining but if you have passion for what you're doing, you'll be able to enjoy yourself even through the boring stuff.

5. Passion is the bridge to success.
Every successful person started their journey with something that motivated them. Something that made them passionate. The beauty of success is that there are millions of ways to make money and it's certainly best for you if you find a way to make money doing something you love. Whether it's an idea, a thought, or a dream you want to fulfill, a real passion for life will inspire you through into success. If you lack love and the charge to succeed, you'll probably turn your attention somewhere else with time.

"I have no special talents. I am only passionately curious."
-Albert Einstein

Chapter 2: Simplify Your Life

Simplification is the perfect tool for when you feel like you're journey to success is becoming far to complicated.

As you start your adventure, you begin to pick up ideas, systems, actions and strategies that you can use to make a wonderful impact inside of your life but over the course of a couple months and a couple years, you begin to become overwhelmed with the complexity that success can bring.

As you already know successful people are passionate and passionate people tend to engage heavily in what sparks them.

That's great news for you because these highly driven professionals become a great resource to learn from. Successful people love to share what helped them make it to the top and they'd love nothing more than for you to make it.

That's pretty cool! But it also leaves you in a bind every once in a while to where you're far too overwhelmed to do anything with the information you've learned and your left completely paralyzed with information overload.

Information Overload

In modern day, information overload is becoming more and more relevant. We're now in what theorists are projecting to become the information age. An era in human civilization in which we acquire, collect, learn and use information and use your mind to make a living.

Our wold is shifting from a labor intensive world into a territory that's unfamiliar to the human race. A life time filled with contemplation and thought. We're beginning to use your minds in exchange for shelter, food and luxuries rather than our labor.

This has led to an incredible amount of information being produced and it's literally impossible for one person to currently handle.

Our technology is consistently updating us with notifications from our favorite sites, our friends, news feeds and updates from around the world. Our friends and families can contact us through fast mediums that directly go to the palm of your hand.

Combined with the necessity to keep up with information, engaging with your loved ones and even learn new things that you need to apply to your goals, dreams and to your character; your mind can quickly overload and paralyze your ability to take action, think fluently and progress.

The cure for this is simplification:

Simplification

"Everything should be made as simple as possible, but not simpler."

- Albert Einstein

Simplification is the art and science of allowing yourself to break down complex problems and to identify the easiest way for both addressing a problem and creating a solution.

Here are some simple ways to begin simplifying your life.

1. Understand that you are the only person in control of designing your life. People are born unique and have been programmed with free will. It's within our nature to be able to create and design your own life. Recognizing that you are truly the ruler of your life and you are in control of your designs will begin to allow you to know what information to pay attention to and what information to pass up on.

It is your responsibility to design your life and you can't use any excuses to stop you from living the lifestyle you choose.

2. Identify what takes up most of your attention. By finding out where your attention takes you by observing how you spend your day, you'll be able to rapidly be able to develop a system where you can make time for yourself. Dedicate times in your day for the things that drain your attention over the course of your week.

Examples include: TV between 5-6, Checking your email in small windows, spending 15 minutes a day on social media. Have windows that you completely dedicate to learning and windows that you entirely dedicate to taking actions to become successful.

3. Stop multi-tasking.

Multi-tasking is the ultimate killer of production. Productivity robs us of what really matters in life. Being present within your moment and focusing on the task at hand. By working on two things at once, your mind shifts gears consistently and although you finish two tasks at once, LOOSE 40% OF YOUR PRODUCTION. This production robs you of the little time you have to produce every day. So stop trying to do 2 or more things at once and knock things out of the ballpark one at a time. You'll be able to free up your time so you can spend even more time doing the things you love.

4. Re-evaluate your relationships.

It's a well known fact that you are the sum of the 5 people you spend the most of your time with.

So it's important to ask yourself, which people inside of your life are being toxic? Are they draining your energy, are they trying to discourage you or control you?

What can you do about fixing the toxic aspects of your relationship?

It's important that once you get a grasp on your goals and you start consistently achieve what you set out to do that the people around you should be there to help support you and allow you to succeed.

You'll quickly find out that as you simplify your life that you don't have time for a bunch of overly complicated situations and that you're being distracted from what ultimately matters in life. Being happy and becoming successful.

By curbing back time that you spend with people and shifting your schedule around, you'll drastically simplify your life and allow yourself to focus on what truly matters. Your success. If your loved ones are there for you and support you along the way, you're in luck! But life isn't always that easy. It's important to eliminate your distractions and to sit down, relax and focus on becoming more successful.

5. Shut off your technology for 30 minutes a day.

Set an alarm, turn your phone on silent and shut off your computer, your TV and your tablet. Simply be present inside of your moment and eliminate every distraction in your life.

Taking a digital detox every day will allow your mind to recenter and regroup. Simply by pausing from the consistent pulsing of information that enters your life every 15 minutes will allow you to just sit, relax and reconnect back into ourselves. You can even spend your time outside with friends and family if you'd like. The important part is just to unplug your information for a while.

Your mind will thank you

6. Still your mind. A lot of people really don't like the thought of sitting down for 15 minutes and being completely still with all absent of thought. However, this absolute waste of time in which you literally do nothing will quickly become a gem inside of your life.

Stilling your mind will allow you to simplify your life to incredible levels.

Just a few benefits are you'll stop that looping pattern that you've been thinking or feeling about for a while. You'll gain a superior control over your mind(at least in spurts of 15 minutes.). And you'll even be able to approach your life from a new angle through more basic thoughts.

The truth is, stilling your mind makes your mind create more productive thoughts because it only has a limited time in which it can operate. By holding your attention to nothing, you'll be able to think of easy fixes to the problems that you feel complicated.

    7. Kill your to-do list.

By killing your to dos you're simplifying your mind in a way that allows you to breath.

Let go of the things that you're suppose to do this week and really only focus on the necessities. Yes you have to pick up food, go to work and pay your bills but a lot of things that you feel obligated to do, might be needlessly complicating your life.

Switch things up for a week and build a list of things you want to do and LITERALLY replace them with the to do list you had before. Not everything will stick but it'll certainly allow you to simplify your life and re-evaluate the commitments you put to the table week in and week out.

    8. Consciously simply tasks for your career. Work provides us with a never ending set of tasks

that may never get done but through the power of simplification, you can streamline your work flow. The perfect way to simplify your work flow is by focusing on essential tasks and accomplishing them at the beginning of your day and your week so you can spend the second half of your day or week on mindless busy tasks that fill up your work.

9. Learn how to say no. Unlike the movie Yes Man, it's completely cool to say no to opportunities that present themselves in your life. Life is more simple and more manageable if you focus on what matters most to you. If you're friends are going out, it's fine to pass.

10. Organize your computer and delete all of your clutter. If you have emails or notifications that you get that you honestly don't need or thoroughly enjoy, just eliminate it. Decluttering how often you get notifications will make your important notifications actually worthy of notice.

11. Ask yourself what a simple life is to you? What would you enjoy about a simple life? Then, simply do it.

12. Work on one, simple goal at a time. It's understandable if you want to accomplish about 127 things by the end of the year but working on 1, important simple goal will transform your life. Look at what you want to do in your life and where you are currently. Ask yourself what SIMPLE and very specific goal would transform my life the most? Once you get the answer, work on that specific goal until you accomplish it and then more on to the next goal!

Chapter 3: Prioritize Your Life

When you set out on your mission to become successful, you become responsible for everything inside of your life and it can quickly become overwhelming.

Have no fear. Not everything in life can get done and it's probably far more important to put off the things that are currently stressing out. If you ran a multi million dollar company and you HAD to work 10 hours a day to keep it running, how would you organize your life?

Sometimes it feels like there's no way you could possibly make it through the sea of actions you need to surf through.

Finishing everything on your plate is impossible if you're ambitious BUT when you first become successful, you'll learn the power that project management create inside of your life.

When you begin to tackle bigger tasks, you'll notice that you'll naturally plug in smaller tasks in places you'd never expect. Becoming good at prioritization is a crucial fundamental to success. Prioritizing helps spark critical decision making skills while simultaneously increasing your productivity into incredible heights.

But how in the world do you actually prioritize?

1. **Answer what will make the biggest impact inside of your life?**

When you're plate is stacked with bottomless sushi, you still have to start somewhere.

A perfect way to prioritize is to simply ask yourself what actions will make the biggest impact in my life and how do I apply them in the quickest fashion?

You really need to break things down and just get to work.

Success isn't about doing a million things like a well oiled billionaire.

It's about identifying what's simple actions you can take that will have the biggest impact inside of your life.

Then, just leave some things on the plate. Even if you really want to hangout with your loved ones or go to a concert, it doesn't mean that you must. Make room to become successful and over time your success will return the favor by making room for the things you love.

2. **Ask other successful people how they manage complicated tasks.** Odds are if you're looking to become successful you have access to somebody who has a ton of things to do every day and every once in a while you'll realize how simplistic your life is.

Asking for feedback from successful people is an incredible way to help simplify your life. What could be thought of as complex systems at the surface could be incredibly easy to manage down at the core and could open up dozens of hours for you every week. Regardless of what you're facing, someone has conquered it unless you're Elon Musk trying to send 1 million people to Mars, someone's probably already conquered the challenges that you are facing. Do yourself a favor and ask for a little help or do a little research to simplify things!

3. Working backwards.

Working backwards is an amazing way to help you grasp what you need to do in the present moment. Sometimes we are at a lost for what do next. If we work take the tasks we are trying to accomplish and see them as they are finished by a specific deadline, your mind will automatically start to work in new ways. You'll automatically think of new ideas because your mind will have connected your tasks in a different way after it sees the product finished. Whenever you're struggling on how to set up your life or you work flow, prioritizing through taking your finished product and working backwards is a perfect way to spark new ways to do things.

4. Delegate.

It's easy to let our tasks at hand to spiral out of control but we sometimes forget that we can delegate huge chunks of time with friends, hired hands and family. You're busy and you undoubtedly work hard so why try to find actions that can be taken that include other people?

Over a life time, delegation can save you a couple years of time. Whether you hire people to do busy work or even tackle big problems, you'll find that the less you have to do, the more you can focus on projects that you need to.

Delegation is one of the finest tricks to prioritization. It's probably good at becoming great at surrounding yourself with people who can do an extraordinary amount for you.

Chapter 4: Live Outside Your Comfort Zone

Breaking outside of your comfort zone could be more difficult than changing habits but putting yourself in an uncomfortable position will have massive effects on your ability to create success inside of your life. Even though it can be challenging to mix up, there's actually a scientific reason to how breaking your comfort zone is so difficult. If you're not careful, your comfort zone will take you to the grave with a very average outcome.

When things are going well, it's very easy to get complacent and to love your life but with a few adjustments you can very easily break free of your comfort zone and put yourself in an extraordinary position to succeed.

So why is it nice to get familiar with your routines and to become comfortable with how life is now? What's so wrong with loving what you have at the moment right?
Answering these questions can be a bit of a challenge but stay patient because this tool is a wonderful way to create a rapidly more successful life.

The real reason why being comfortable is so dangerous.

Your comfort zone is known to psychologists as a behavioral space that you place your actions and routines inside of a world where you live with the least amount of stress possible. This is also known as the path of least resistance. The path of least resistance gives us the incredible benefits of mental security along with the lovely emotions of happiness and reduced anxiety.

This is truly where you want to be in life right? So why are you trying to break down the stability you worked so hard in your life to earn?

Well to better understand that, it's best to flash back into an experiment in the year 1908. Mr. Robert Yerkes and the legendary John Dodson indicated through their studies that your comfort zone allows you to perform at a very static level.

However, in order to maximize your performance level, you need to induce a higher level of stress. This state is known as optimal anxiety and creates superstars from ordinary people.

But be careful, too much stress will shut your ability to focus and your nervous system completely down and you'll be stuck in flight or fight mode.

The goal is to put your body inside of a state where it has to work harder to keep itself in the same comfortable condition.

Successful careers and businesses thrive off of optimal anxiety.

It's a hack that allow you to really challenge yourself and to exceed your wildest expectations. Leaving your comfort zone has been a really exciting point of contact for psychologists over the past century because of the delicate balance of focus that specific stress level puts you under.

It's incredibly hard to master from the beginning but it's well worth the focus if you're trying to become successful.

It's not about putting yourself in a condition where if you fail, your life comes crashing to the ground but it does use the delicate art of leveraging to accomplish a performance level that you never would have expected from yourself.

If you've ever crammed for a test or had to make a little extra money last minute, you'll probably look back and think "wow, I definitely was impressive during that stretch!"

But then, you naturally put yourself into that natural state of relaxation until you need to pull out your tricks the next time you're in a tad bit of trouble. Once you understand how your Optimal Anxiety works, it's really easy to see how understand why it's so hard to kick your brain out of your comfort zone. Well the good news is if you put your body in this condition on a consistent basis, you don't send your body into stress that's unbearable and you don't induce cancer inside of your body.

Your comfort zone is something that can easily trap you and hold you back, but by mastering the art of making yourself just a tad bit uncomfortable, you begin to take your goals and your success into new heights that you never would have expected before you used Optimal Anxiety.

What happens when you leave your comfort zone.

Optimal Anxiety puts your body at the perfect level of mental production and it's known as being in "The Zone" or can also be called flow.

This peak performance allows you to produce at all star levels on a consistent basis and is the same exact state of mind that professional athletes are going.

So enough with the talk, here's some measurable results you'll create once you apply optimal anxiety into your life.

1. **You'll develop a fluent work flow**

The death of productivity is comfort. This is what we encounter in a world where we have no deadlines or expectations inside of your work schedule or throughout your week. When we don't have to push to do produce anything, it actually causes us to look away from what we should be doing and makes us even less productive than when we put the pressures of deadlines into our lives.

When we get comfortable, we loose that drive within us to become better and we begin to disengage from our contemplations and work through automatic habit in a relaxing manner. We lose the drive and ambition to do more and learn new things. When we first start a job, it's typical for us to work hard to put ourselves in a good position and that work flow completely evaporates if we're not careful. We quickly fall into that work trap and our work flow becomes boring and dull.

By always pushing yourself to get better and put yourself into a better position and produce better results, you're actually placing a slight form of optimal anxiety onto yourself rather than settle for your current position in life.

If you want to become more successful, set the goal of getting a promotion and become the best in the company at what you do. Establish a work flow and push yourself into a position that you have to succeed at a further level.

2. **You'll adapt really quickly to sudden changes inside your life.**

By taking controlled risks you'll quickly begin challenging yourself into things that you never would have done while you were chilling inside of your comfort zone. Hitting the frontier to the furthest place you've ever been will be the perfect way to help us embrace for sudden changes that happen inside of our lives. Life truly is a box of chocolates but they don't always taste delicious.

By consistently pushing yourself out of your comfort zone, you'll be able to react to the times that your home or environment becomes unstable. This allows you to be able to stay grounded instead of stress out and make matters worse.

3. **The more you break barriers now the easier you can break them in the future.**

The moment you step outside of your comfort zone and you survive the journey, you'll begin to quickly embrace what the strategy brings to your life.

The even better news is that once you step outside of you comfort zone for a while, it gets easier. Over time, you'll end up making huge progress inside of your life.

This theory is called productivity discomfort. Once you get a nice taste of this "discomfort" you'll begin to push yourself further every day and you'll reach new heights with even less stress than you originally had when you began using optimal anxiety.

4. Optimal Anxiety sparks creativity

Although optimal anxiety boosts your creativity, it's thought to be a mild benefit that you can utilize in the tool for success.

It's well known that pushing yourself out of your comfort zone forces you to learn new things and connect new associations inside of your life and your career. You'll begin to speak differently and become more fluent in your thoughts and your life.

The things that use to stress you out before tend to automatically fix themselves and you'll be able to open more doors than you thought possible. Pushing out of our comfort zone makes us reflect on new things and even puts us Trying new things can make us reflect on our old ideas and where they clash with our new knowledge, and inspire us to learn more and experience new things.

But how in the world do we actually break out of the cozy living we're accustomed to?

Strategies that break you out of your comfort zone.
As long as you stay within reasonable boundaries, always being slightly uncomfortable is the best habit you could ever create inside of your lifestyle.

However, It's important to understand that there is a huge difference between manipulating your anxiousness and sending yourself into a spiraling anxiety attack. If you push the limits too far, you'll drop off the fragile cliff of optimal anxiety and you'll wreck your mental capacity and your nervous system.

Everyone's comfort zone is unique and everyone responds to different stresses in a different manner. It's important to use this strategy inside of your life if you'd like to be optimally successful but at the same time, your goal isn't to stress yourself out of your mind. It's incredibly unhealthy and there are real damaging side effects to going over board.

Here's a few tricks to get you started moving out of your cozy lifestyle and into something new.

1. **Mix up your every day tasks**.

A cool way to get yourself out of your comfort zone is to switch up your routs across town. Go see a movie without checking it out or attend something new like an art gallery or a restaurant. Try cleaning up your house by using a different style or cooking up something new. Buy a new gadget you've never used before or check out some software you've never seen. You could even go on a hike, a walk, or even a new workout routine. Simply mix up the way you spend your life. It's a perfect way to move out of your comfort zone without adding in high stress volumes into your life.

2. Develop a new way to make your decisions.

Sometimes we breeze through decisions that could have a lot more consequences than what we account for. If you slow down and actually contemplate simple decisions that you make on a day to day basis, you'll very quickly push yourself out of your comfort zone. Every once in a while, it's great to pause and really look at the implications your choices make impact your life on a bigger scale. By analyzing the little things, you'll be making more educated decisions more often and you'll put yourself out of your cozy day to day life.

3. Trust your intuition to make massive decisions.

It could take months and even years for you to make major decisions inside of you life. And after all that time, you're still confused about what to do.

Life is a huge adventure of mistakes and success but what's most important is making your monumental decisions quickly, sicking by them and seeing where it takes you.

Life is filled with risk no matter what you do so when it comes to massive decisions, use your intuition to quickly make your choice and stick by it. Jumping into something that has taken you years to decide will undoubtedly put you out of your comfort zone.

4. Take it slow

When your learning how to step outside of your comfort zone, it's important to take it slow. It takes a lot of inspiration and bravery to break out of your perfectly content shell so don't try to do too much too fast. Try to take on little tasks at work and challenge yourself to develop a new skill. It's alright to ease your way into things to see how you react and figure out what you react well to and what tends to over stress you. Break out into taking on new responsibilities but don't take over more than you can handle.

Whether it's learning a second language or learn how to program software or build a website. Maybe take on traveling. If you've spent your entire life one small area maybe you should go on a plane flight to some distant land you've never encountered. Whatever you do that's new will be enough to put you in an incredible work flow by the time you get back to work.

Chapter 5: The Golden Rule

"Do unto others as you would have them do unto you."

This is a very significant rule to live by the golden rule. Unfortunately most people do not follow this. People expect you to treat them with respect, but wont hesitate to show no respect to others.

It is not a difficult to be nice to everyone. It can feel like a natural thing, if you truly mean it, and why not truly mean it? You never know what some one is going through. Some one could be considering suicide, and you being kind to them could save their life. Or even something that not as serious, maybe they got into a fight with their significant other and are feeling down. Every little bit of kindness can go such a long way. And you don't even know it.

If you show respect to others, then they admire you for it. Leading by example is always a good thing to do. People tend to follow, and why not give them something good to follow?

With all these negative role models that are in the world today, you could impact some one in just a little way by being nice.

Plus if you are having a bad day yourself, and you shoot a smile at everyone you see. It will brighten your own day.

As Gandhi has said **"Be the change you wish to see in the world."**

If you want to see a change in the world, you have to do something to put into it. When you are good to others, it inspires them to do the same. Why not put kindness into some ones heart? Some people need it more than you think, and their families could as well. Its like a chemical reaction.

We are all humans being. **"One is all, and all is one" Edward Elric.** Everything is linked together. The food chain, human life, the earth. If we started treating every single people with how we would treat ourselves. Do you know how great the world could be?

"Be kind, for everyone you meet is fighting a harder battle."
 Plato

Imagine how wonderful, and peaceful the world could be if we all lived by the golden rule. If you treat everyone with respect, and kindness you will receive that kindness in return. Although, not every person you meet is nice and some people let their lives be consumed by anger. Do not let that affect you, kill them with kindness. Maybe even something as little as that could change their mindset. Even if you never get to see the change it could do. You can at least sleep better at night knowing you were still nice.

If you are more empathetic to other people, it will be easy for you to be kind. Really try to understand what they are going through. This will help you have better relationships with your friends and family.

Be compassionate towards every one you meet. Try to feel what they are going through and try to help the end to their suffering.

Always consider how you want to be treated, and always treat others the same way. It is not fair to do something to some one that you would not want done to you. No one likes a hypocrite. Also take into consideration of how they want to be treated as well. Their is always comprise, especially in a relationship. Every one has different ideas on how they want to be treated. Sit down and talk to that person and try to understand them.

Be helpful when you can, this is a weakness that society suffers from as well. Never let some one take advantage of you, always be able to recognize that. Yet being helpful when it is necessary, and would benefit the person is always fine.

Always make sure to listen to others, We always seem to want to talk, but so many people just needs some one to listen to them. In a world where every body feels the need to always have to express their opinion, make sure every one is heard.

Never judge some one, every one has a different way of living life. So let them live it, if it is not life harming and they are doing what they want to be happy.

Do not be prejudice, not matter what skin color some one has, or what they look like, we are all human beings and every one should be treated equally.

Everyone has different ways of thinking, and even if you disagree with them you should not disrespect them for how they chose to think. Telling some one how to act or what to do is very controlling. Every one should be able to have a free spirit.

Try to have a child like mentality, they accept every one for who they are, and love every one equally. They are always so happy, and nice to every person they meet.

If some one is being rude to you, try not to retaliate. Two wrongs do not make a right, resist the urge. You will feel better knowing you did not let that person get to you. Regardless of how they have treated you, you're being the bigger person and showing what kindness can really do. It does not mean you should be a doormat, some people step over the line, but there is calm way to approach certain situations.

You will feel so much better treating others with love, trust and respect. When people feel compassion from others they can't but help let the demons subside within them, and calm down. They will see what is going on more clearly and the situation will go a lot better.

You will notice changes within yourself. You will feel happier and more at peace.

So always try to remember how important this rule is. Energy can spread like a wild fire, and if you go to everyone you meet with kindness, they will spread it even father. Always live by everything that was written here. What I have wrote will guide you to staying true to the golden rule. Always treat others how you would want to be treated. Your loved ones will appreciate you for it, and even random strangers you meet along the way.

Chapter 6: Always Keep Learning

Lifelong learning is the power of heavy engagement and contemplation inside of your mind that allows you to keep your neurons firing and your brain cells active. Whether or not we set out to be knowledge warriors, it's now supported by science that lifelong learning is healthy and the lack of learning is devastating to our mental health.

Evidence now supports that people are just as capable of learning and retaining advanced information when they grow older as when they are children.

This finding suggests that our minds never stop the ability to learn until we stop and that the longer we engage inside of our brain, the more healthy we'll be with time.

There's a saying that says by the time you finish learning your degree, it already becomes obsolete.

Today's business world is incredibly fast paced and evolving at a level that's unknown to man. The only way to conquer this ever changing environment is to always keep yourself on top of the knowledge inside of your industry and to apply what you're learning.

Just a couple decades ago, it was easy to sit down,

go to school and walk away with a high paying career for the rest of your life. Once you put in that hard work, all the days of learning your craft and improving seemed like a challenge that wasn't worth up keeping. Sadly times have changed but you can still use that to your advantage.

By maintaining a hold inside of your field, the more we can offer our employer and your bosses actually give incentives to stay up to date with the newest strategies and information. If you look into it, you'll be surprised at what your company offers. They'll pay for more school and send you to conferences across the world. You'll be able to study new certifications and strategies and your employer loves every minute of it.

By continuously learning, you'll keep your mind young, engaged and even spark innovation inside of your business and your career. Ideas are what customers and employers both find valuable. Anything that improves your business profits or improve production has your career in an upswing.

The most successful people in the world believe that reading and learning is the ultimate advantage but where should you start?
Well start with just a simple commitment to reading and learning anywhere from a 30 minutes to a couple hours a day. Use your curiosity to your advantage and always use the position that you're currently in to create a better circumstance for yourself through the acquisition of knowledge.

You can focus on expanding your vocabulary or even becoming more persuasive. Character building is a

wonderful place to learn about tools that you've never discovered through formal education.
If you haven't studied business much maybe venture there. You can learn business analytics and business strategy to sure up the production in your goals and allow you to become even more successful.

You can even dive in to learn something you're truly passionate about. Whatever you choose to do, make sure you set aside just a little bit of time every day to help invigorate your mind and keep you young and fresh.

"Intellectual growth should commence at birth and cease only at death."

- Albert Einstein

Chapter 7: Living With Gratitude

"Happiness cannot be traveled to, owned, earned, worn or consumed. Happiness is the spiritual experience of living every minute with love, grace, and gratitude." Denis Waitley

Life with out gratitude can barely be life at all. When you are being ambitious its easy to get caught up in the success and forget to give gratitude for the things that are happening in your life.

With out gratitude, with out sending out that positive energy; the good that is happening in your life could stop at any moment. What you put out, is ultimately what you will receive in the end. If you always have humbleness and gratitude in your life, things will keep going well for you.

Giving gratitude to the people that are around you that are helping you thrive is most important. If some one is helping you succeed and reach to goals where you want to be in life, showing them love, grace and gratitude is very important. What would make them want to stay and help you if they don't feel appreciated?

Often in our lives we start to feel sorry for ourselves. We have that attitude of; Why me? Why is this happening to me?

We need to stop so much thinking in the word of "me". Every thing happens for a reason. Some people are in your life to stay, and some are in your life to teach you a lesson. If we start looking in the positive of things that are happening to us, instead of focusing on the negative. Your life will in the end alter in to some thing so happy and amazing.

When you have reached that mentally strong point in your life, you will start having gratitude for every thing that has happened to you.

You will have a more positive outlook, and be able to go on every day like nothing you have been through has even touched you. Pain can hurt, but it does not have to hurt forever.

If you simply take one moment every day to having gratitude, finding the positive in all the negative. You will be able to go to sleep with a smile on your face. That should happen every night regardless of how "hard" your day was.

If you want to become stronger, and be happier. You first have to change your outlook on life. If not you will stay in the same cycle every day. This sadness effects your health, and ultimately will result in a shorter life. And why not live life to the fullest while we have such beauty in it? Why not live when others don't have that choice?

Here are 7 different way that are to improve your gratitude for life, you don't really think about how much this affects every day life. If you live your life by this, there is no way you can not succeed in your dreams. But the most important things, live the rest of your days happy.

1. **Gratitude can brings new relationships into your life:** Showing people that you are friendly brings new relationships to your life. If you feel lonely you can't expect people to confront you if you're never smiling. So smile and say thank you to people who help you. Even if its just saying thank you for some one holding a door for you. Acknowledging other peoples presences shows them you are caring. This can lead to new adventures you could of never had with out meeting that person. Every thing you want is on the other side of fear.

2. **Gratitude helps you feel better physically:** When you are down and depressed about life, you are less likely to get up and properly take care of yourself. A study in 2012 proved that if you show gratitude for your life, you're most likely to get up and work out and get check ups. We are blessed to live the life we have. Why not take care of ourselves? You have more energy, and just smile more when your body feels good.

3. **Gratitude will improve your empathy and reduce your anger:** When you are more grateful in you're life, it is less likely that you will let some one

ruin your day. Every had one negative comment just ruin your day? Even if it was from a complete stranger? Have gratitude will give you more confidence, even when you get negative feedback. You will be less likely to seek revenge, whats the point of trying to ruin some one days just because they were rude to you? There is no point, and that's the truth. Let them go on in that negative mindset, and you can walk away with a smile. You will feel more sensitive towards these people, and maybe consider they are just having a bad day. Your act of kindness could turn their attitude around. Even if you do not witness it.

4. **When you are grateful you will sleep better:** If you are more grateful for things in your life, you will have so much less to stress about. That's what usually keeps us up at night. If you take a journal every night before bed and write what you are grateful for, I can guarantee you will sleep much better, and longer.

5. **Gratitude will help improve your self-esteem:** Comparison is the thief of joy. If you are more grateful for your life, you can appreciate what others have accomplished instead of being envious and then hating your own life. This decreases your self esteem and why would you do that to yourself? You are worth every ounce of self esteem and happiness. If you are grateful for your whole being and what you have, nothing can stop you. And nothing should. The day you stop comparing your life to others you will see such a difference. You are not that person, you are yourself. How could you expect your life to go exactly as their has? Set your own goals, do your

own things. Be happy about it, and go out there and do what you want to do.

6. **Gratitude will increase your mental strength:** Being grateful during times of trauma, is the most important thing you could do for yourself. It will ultimately make you mentally stronger in the end. Like I said before every thing happens for a reason, and you can not change what has happened, so why dwell on it? Take the lessons from what had happened to you, and let it transform you into a better person. Why let life beat you down when you can strive from it and do better? You are ruining your life when you let every thing affect you so personally. Reach beyond the troubles, and sky rocket above.

7. **Gratitude will improve your psychological health:** Living life with resentment and envy does not help any thing. Its like letting that person who hurt you in some way live in your head rent free. These are nasty feelings that no one likes to feel, so why would you succumb yourself to that negativity? Having gratitude for your life and the people around you will greatly decrease you depression, and increase your happiness. Just try it and see, you will love yourself for it.

You may think your life has been to bad to live with gratitude and that is just not true. Every single one of us has to ability to change our way of thought. If you spend less time complaining and talking positively, the unhappiness will stop. You will have to work for it, but wont it be worth it in the end? Every thing always is. Having gratitude is a simple way to improve your satisfaction with life.

Life can be filled with glorious things. Going to different countries, meeting new people. If you did not live your life to the fullest, you will miss out on so much. Instead of just doing things just because you have too, savor the moment, rejoice in it. Smiling is the best thing you can do for yourself. At first it might be forced, but not after long it will come to your face with ease.

If you want to inspire yourself, look up some quotes to help you through your struggles. Look up your roles models and see what they have done to improve their own life. Gratitude come from what you manifest, surround your self with positive things, and eventually it will glue to you like nothing. If you feel more passionate and driven you will get so much done in a day. You will see how much you can really do when you are happy, and have ambition.

You have the powerful the control your thoughts. If you're thinking negative, acknowledge the thought, then just let it float away. Tell your mind thank you, but you do not need this negative, and just let it be. Tell your conscious mind, that being positive is more important than focusing on the negative.

Any words that make you feel useless or stressed out, stop them. Replace them with more positive thinking. You're the only person that knows what goes on in your head, and only you can stop it. You know yourself better than any one does, so find something that works for you and stick to it.

Always appreciate what you have, do not focus on what you don't have. If you really want it, work for it! You can not expect your life to get better if you sit around and do nothing with it. Follow through with every thing you want to do to improve yourself. Any thing is possible with the right mind set.

Helping others will help you feel better as well. Giving aid to others is one of the most rewarding things you can do. Being selfless is the best feeling of all. Even the simple things count. Saying hi to a stranger, helping an elderly person with their groceries. Anything that is a selfless act with make you feel better.

Only you have the power to fill your life with gratitude. Don't ever let any one tell you otherwise. Keep those negative people out of your life, all they will do is bring you down. Stay with this mind set, and you will see in no time how much it improves your life. Our lives can be so short some times, so why waste a day unhappy when you can live your life to the fullest?

"Gratitude unlocks the fullness of life. It turns what we have into enough, and more. It turns denial into acceptance, chaos to order, confusion to clarity. It can turn a meal into a feast, a house into a home, a stranger into a friend." Melody Beattie

www.ingramcontent.com/pod-product-compliance
Lightning Source LLC
Chambersburg PA
CBHW070334190526
45169CB00005B/1893